THE DISTRICT SIX MUSEUM FOUNDATION

published by the
District Six Museum
First Edition 1999
Second Edition 2001
Third Edtition 2002
Fourth Edition 2003
Fifth Edition 2005
Sixth Edition 2007

ISBN: 0-620-24720-7

Reproduction by Scan Shop
cover design: Haajirah Esau, Jos Thorne
design and layout: Jos Thorne

The Museum Workshop

To Jen and Phil. with best wishes. from Noor Ebrahim 12-11-2008

NOOR'S STORY

My Life in District Six

Isgaak, Noor, Hoosain, Mother Zohra, Father Gasant, Mariam, Gowah, Gabeba

Noor Ebrahim

District Six in the early 1960s

Photo: Ridwaan Jattiem

CONTENTS

Images on this page are reproduced form "The Puppet Theatre" by Sandra Macgregor. (District Six Museum Collection)

NOOR'S STORY

This is my story and the story of my family. We grew up and lived in District Six, an area of approximately one and a half square kilometres, which spread along the flank of Table Mountain south of the centre of Cape Town. District Six was given this name in 1867 because it was then the sixth municipal district in Cape Town. It was originally a mixed community of freed slaves, immigrants, labourers, merchants and artisans. Later it included a different kind of mix – artists, politicians, businessmen, musicians, writers, teachers, sheikhs, priests, gangsters, sportsmen, housewives and always lots of children.

Sixty to seventy thousand people lived together in great harmony until disaster struck our community.

THE BOMBSHELL

On the 11th of February 1966 District Six was officially declared an area for white people only. This is one day I will never forget. The newspapers were filled with the news. District Six buzzed with talk about its future. Friends and family began to worry about how life would change. The uncertainty made me feel empty. But nothing happened immediately and after the initial shock life went on as usual.

It was nine years later in 1975 that the darkness descended on my family. One evening on my way home from work, I saw bulldozers demolishing houses and shops in William,

Stone (which we knew as "Klip") and Caledon Streets. I knew that I was witnessing a terrible evil. I felt hopeless and helpless. Day after day, the bulldozers came closer to our house. Too soon it was our turn. Officials of the government told me that I had one month in which to clear out. What could I do? No one had any choice in the matter. I made arrangements to buy a house in Athlone. Luckily our children Isgaak and Mariam were too young to fully understand what was happening.

On the final day the lorry that I hired was loaded with our furniture. My wife and children crowded into the Beetle with our belongings. I drove away from Caledon Street and then stopped the car in the middle of the road. I had to turn back. I had to look at the house one more time.

Yet I could not end it there. On my way to the Reader's Digest office, where I worked, I drove down Caledon Street past my house. Each day for six days, I stopped my car and stared at my house. On the seventh day I got out of the car, leaned against it for a moment and then walked around the house. By now the windows and window frames had been removed. The front door still carried the small round royal blue and white plate indicating that this was 247 Caledon Street. I ran at the door and ripped off our number. Then I went to the kitchen and saw that the bolt was still on the back door. I removed this too and took it with me. A week later I passed my street again and saw that the house was gone. Even the rubble had been removed. I stood on the vacant plot with desolation in my heart.

It was at this time that my brother Hoosain and I bought a Voigtlander camera. It cost us thirty-eight rand but it was worth it (or at thirty-eight rand it was a bargain). We wanted to capture scenes from what was left of District Six before it disappeared completely. Most of the photographs in this book I took during this period.

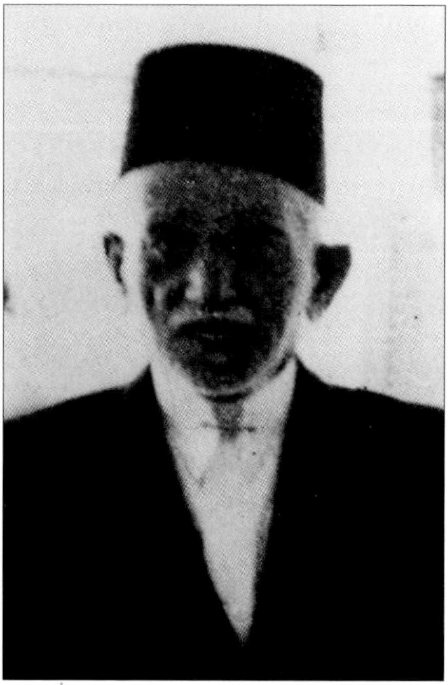

My Grandfather
Mohammed Hoosain Ebrahim

My Grandmother
Mariam Ebrahim

MY GRANDFATHER

My grandfather came to District Six towards the end of the 19th century. He came from Surat, a town not far from Bombay. He established a general dealer's shop in District Six and by 1920, a ginger beer factory in Dreyer Street, Claremont.

My grandfather's first wife was a woman called Mariam Ebrahim (née Fanny Grainger) who was Scottish. Together they produced a family of nine sons and two daughters. He took Mariam to Mecca in 1922. She died there. On his return from Mecca, he approached a friend and asked permission to marry his daughter. She too was named Mariam. Her surname was Hendricks and she was eighteen years old. She bore four sons and five daughters. She died in 1939. My grandfather then married a third wife. She was also eighteen years old. Her name was Mymoena Kriel. They had one son, Sharief. My grandfather left Mymoena and married a fourth wife, Kaltoema Dollie, and he had two children with her. He died in 1954 when I was 10 years old.

After my grandfather's second wife died he bought a house in Princess Street, Walmer Estate. He moved there with his third wife Mymoena, while some of his children (including my father) continued living at his home in 247 Caledon Street. Although some of his twenty children were married by this time, the oldest single child took care of the younger ones.

Some of his children worked at the ginger-beer factory.

My grandfather's name was Mohamed Hoosain Ebrahim but he was popularly known as Hadjee Peerbhai. He became a well-known businessman and religious leader. After small beginnings he eventually imported sugar, rice and ginger for the brewing of ginger beer. He also owned many properties in District Six: a double-storey (commercial building?) in Balmoral Street and another in Ayre Street; two houses in Clifton Street; eight houses in Rose Street; 2 Combrinck Street and 4 Cross Street. Always active as a religious leader, he used to organise *hadj* trips on an Italian liner to the Muslim holy city of Mecca.

When I was eight years old I often went with my father to the ginger-beer factory. The ginger-beer was made in huge wooden barrels. Long wooden spoons were used to stir the mixture. I had to climb three wooden steps to look into the barrels and there were times when I was allowed to take the wooden spoon and stir the mixture. The "Peerbhai Ginger Beer" bottles were filled from taps on the barrels and sealed with corks. Then they were placed in crates and transported from the factory in Claremont to our house in Caledon Street. From there my father and his brothers would deliver the ginger-beer to the people's houses.

MY FATHER

When my father left District Six in 1974 he had the option of buying or renting a house in Mitchells Plain. Instead, he decided to buy a house in Primrose Park through the Department of Community Development, an organisation set up by the government to oversee the forced removals. My wife, our two young children and I were still in the house in Caledon Street. My father missed his old home terribly. Every day he drove in to Cape Town in his white Volkswagen Beetle, to drop my brother Isgaak off at work,

My Father, my Aunt Hadjira sitting on the chair and my cousin Faldiela on her lap

My home in District Six

and then he would drive up to our house in Caledon Street and park there. Dressed in a suit and tie and wearing his red fez, he would walk the streets of District Six all day long until it was time to collect Isgaak. When he was not walking the streets, my father would go to the Muir Street Mosque to pray, visit his remaining friends at the mosque or visit our home in Caledon Street.

Even after our house was demolished and the rubble removed, my father continued dropping Isgaak at work and spending hours at the Muir Street Mosque. By 1974 many more people had been forced out of their homes. The destruction of our neighbourhood was advancing daily. It was only when the area became devastated that my father stopped visiting District Six.

It took him years to adjust to living in Primrose Park.

My father Gasant, sister Mariam and mother Zohra

MY MOTHER

My mother Zohra Rhoda and her family lived in the Strand. Mammie, as we called her, had one brother and four sisters. She was a friendly person, always available to visit those in need of company or help. She liked crocheting baby clothes and visiting new mothers at the Peninsula Maternity Hospital in District Six. When mothers returned home from the hospital she was usually the first to visit them.

My cousins from the Strand worked in Cape Town. They lived in our house during the week and went home at weekends. My mother treated them like her own children.

Mammie had a few special friends. One was Sis Gawa who lived next door to us at 249 Caledon Street. When we were short of money Mammie would confide in Sis Gawa and she would send us vegetables and fruit.

Mammie loved going to the bioscope but she never went alone. Her two friends, Sis Mariam from 39 Clifton Street and Gadija de Wet of Lewis Street, always went with her. They had their very own permanent seats – row "L"' numbers

12,13 and 14 at the Star Bioscope. They would go on Monday and Saturday nights.

Whenever Mammie went to the bioscope, we would wait up for her as she always brought us Messaris potato chips and chocolates on her return. While we were enjoying these treats, she would describe the film she had seen, telling us the story in complete detail. She made it so exciting that we were never sleepy. We loved to listen to her and enjoyed her bioscope nights as much as she did.

MY STORY

I was born in my parents' house at 247 Caledon Street in 1944. I loved the congested streets, familiar faces, voices and sounds, the twinkling view of the bay at night, and the solid presence of Table Mountain every time you raised your eyes. It was home. District Six and its people shaped me, showed me who I was and how I should be if I wanted to get on in life.

We lived in a double-storeyed house that had three bedrooms, a lounge, kitchen and storeroom. The door in the backyard wall faced Horsburg Lane. Our house was attached

to three other semi-detached cottages as well as St Mark's Church, which stood on the corner of Caledon and Clifton Streets. Eight people lived in our house – my parents, my two brothers Hoosain and Isgaak, and three sisters, Gabeba, Mariam and Gowah.

Attached to our house were two extra rooms and a kitchen. Two of my father's brothers lived there. Ismail, a bachelor, was a gardener, and Abduraghmaan (Laan) was a driver. Laan married a woman by the name of Asia, but they separated early in their marriage. My mother Zohra, or "Joggie" as they fondly called her, cooked for them. They were an extension of our family. Uncle Ismail worked for white people, and many times he brought home carriers of old clothes. He was single but he told his employers that he was married with many children and needed old clothes to sell. I had to take these clothes to Aunty Minnie on the Grand Parade. She was a stout lady who sat under the big palm tree where she sold herbs. Most of the money for the clothes was given to my mother for food but I always got a small tip.

There were times when we had no food for supper. After laying the table at 6pm, we would sit at the table with empty plates waiting for our father to bring food. Sometimes we would wait for two hours and the silence was broken by the growling of our empty stomachs. Then we would look at one another and burst out laughing. When we heard the front door open and the sound of tins and bottles heading towards the kitchen, we knew it was tinned fish for supper. We would help our mother prepare the meal. But there were times when we were not so lucky. Then we had to be satisfied with bread and jam for supper. Fortunately, we never went to bed without something in our stomachs. We knew we could go to our neighbours and they would give us food. The people of District Six shared and cared for each other in this way, no matter what colour they were.

PAGE-BOY AT FIVE YEARS

My cousin Fatiema Cromby asked my parents if I could be a page-boy at her wedding. Her sister Gadija, who was also five years old, was to be the flower-girl. I remember the occasion so well. Almost every day I pestered my mother "Mammie, when am I going to be a page-boy?" She would answer, "Mogamad Noor, have patience, it won't be long now." On the Saturday before the wedding, I was told to go to bed early because the wedding was taking place the following day. At five o' clock that Sunday morning I ran to my parents' room demanding my outfit, and was packed off back to bed.

Eventually at 9.30 I was called to get dressed. It was then I discovered that I would be wearing a Jan van Riebeeck costume. It included a hat with a long feather and matching wig. I was bitterly disappointed and started to cry. Even though my mother assured me that I looked very handsome in the outfit, I refused to wear it. She gave me sweets and promised me many things if I stopped crying. Eventually I agreed, partly because she had promised that I could change into a black suit, white shirt and bow-tie for the festivities after the ceremony.

Noor and Gadija Cromby, 1950

SCHOOL

Salie Dollie was one of the residents of District Six and he owned a Muslim School in Frere Street. Classes ranged from Sub A to Standard 3. My Sub A teacher was Mrs Jappie and in Standards 2 and 3 it was Mr Brown, who was of medium height and very well built. Both of them were also residents of District Six and they are still alive as I write. The principal of the Muslim School was Mr Misbach.

Although it was predominantly a Muslim school Christian children also attended. Our neighbour Mrs Elkie owned a shop. She and Mr Brown were very good friends. Mr Brown would sent me to her shop daily to buy his favourite snack, a quarter pound of cheese. When I ran his errand I would charge into my house and my mother would shout, "Mogamad Noor is that you?" and I'd reply, "Yes Mammie it's me, can I get something to eat very quickly I'm in a big hurry." My mother would say "It's a good thing that I don't lock the front door," and I'd reply "Yes it's a good thing because otherwise I must stand and knock on the door and wait for you to find the key to unlock." Mammie would ask "Did you buy cheese again for that teacher of yours, Mr Brown? Isn't he sick from all the cheese yet?"

I would then jump up and down and tell my mother "I'm in a hurry." As soon as she had given me a sandwich or, if I was lucky, a thick slice of cake, I'd grab it and rush out of the door, clutching the cheese in one hand and stuffing my snack into my mouth. As I ran out of the house eating, Mammie would shout "Don't forget to close the front door!" As I ran along I could feel her voice ringing in my ears: "That Mogamad Noor, he never closes the front door, he's always in such a rush. One day I am going to lock the front door and pretend that I'm not at home." But she never did that.

Mr Brown was a story-teller. Every day, 10 minutes before school closed, Mr Brown would tell our class a story. One day he told us a story about two men who were captured on a boat. They were stow-aways. When they were discovered by the captain, they were chained together on the deck.

They were given food and water every day. They stopped drinking the water and instead used it to pour on to the chains in the hope these would break. They did this for six weeks. They became so dehydrated that instead of the chains breaking their arms became thinner and the shackles just fell off. They became excited because now they could escape but, alas, there was nowhere to go. They were in the middle of the ocean and very far away from any land. So they slipped the shackles back on and from then on drank water with their food everyday.

Mr Brown told us stories in episodes. He would stop the story at the most interesting part and tell us that he would continue the story the following day. We never stayed out of school, as we did not want to miss any part of his stories. There was always something to look forward to at school, like the peanut butter on brown bread which we got with a mug of milk. It was my job to dish out milk to the other children.

Each season we also got fresh fruit. In summer it was guavas and bunches of grapes and in winter it was oranges and apples. When Salie Dollie's school was out, the kids ran home to change and eat. Then we had to go to another school, while Christian children played in the streets. This was the religious one where we were taught lessons from the Surat and the Quran by Sheikh Najaar. This school was in a small hall in Smart Lane and it was used solely to teach Muslim children.

SMOKING IN FRONT OF THE DOVER STOVE

After supper, as a youngster of about 10 years, I would wait until everyone went to bed. Then I would sit at the coal stove, take brown paper, roll it into a tight thin roll to resemble a cigarette, light it on the hot coals and puff away. This is how I taught myself to smoke. When I was in standard four I often picked up *toppetjies* (cigarette ends) on my way to school. In my pocket I usually had brown paper. One day during playtime, surrounded by my friends, with my back to the school, I carefully took out the cigarette ends and the brown paper. I emptied the scraps of tobacco, filled the brown paper and made a neat cigarette. I took matches out of my pocket and lit the cigarette, enjoying the first puff. I blew smoke in the air. All of a sudden, everything was dead quiet. I thought this strange and turned around, only to find myself face to face with the school principal, Mr George Golding. He took me to his office and gave me six of the best on my backside. I later learned that it was the principal's son who had squealed on me. I was angry with him for a long time. Mr Serff, my class teacher, gave me a letter for my mother, who gave it to my father. I knew that I was about to receive another hiding. As soon as I heard his wardrobe opening, I knew that my father was taking out his belt. I took my second punishment like a man. This did not stop me from smoking. At the age of 12 I bought my first packet of Max cigarettes. You got 10 in a packet for sixpence. My friends Salie and Abubaker and I used to smoke in the Star Bioscope. I did not go home immediately because I still smelled of cigarette smoke. I had to visit other friends for an hour or two and even eat at their homes, until the smell was gone. I knew that if my mother got a whiff of smoke on me, I would get another beating.

Photo: Fakier Jessa

WAYNIKS CLOTHING SHOP

I still possess a jersey I bought from Wayniks almost 30 years ago. Our school blazers could only be bought from them because of the particular binding around the blazer. Wayniks was known for stocking various school uniforms. It was Mr George Golding of Ashley High Primary School (AHPS) who arranged the contract for Wayniks to sell school uniforms. Because Wayniks had contracts with certain schools in District Six, people could pay off their children's school uniforms through the schools.

PANTOMIMES

When I left the Salie Dollie Primary School at the age of 10, I went to Ashley High Primary School because of their organised activities like sport, athletics, pantomimes and singing. When I was asked to participate in the pantomimes, I was delighted, saying yes immediately and jumping for joy. We had rehearsals every day after school. I was one of the six cats in Puss in Boots. I did not like my costume. It was an all in one tight-fitting cat suit made from stretch cloth. I had no option, however, if I wanted to be in the play. The cat's head was made of plaster of Paris. It was hot and heavy, with small openings for the eyes, nose and mouth. It was a sacrifice to wear the cat's head, but it was worth it. I loved my part in the play.

On opening night, the players had to meet at 7pm I was there at 6pm as I could not contain my excitement. We were very nervous. The minutes slipped slowly by. Eventually our turn came. We had to walk like cats and at the end turn our backs to the audience and wiggle our heavy fat tails from side to side. The audience burst out laughing and the hall resounded with applause.

GAMES

During the marble season, the Babbie shops made money selling marbles to the young boys of District Six. Girls were not supposed to play with marbles as it was strictly a game for boys. If girls did play, they were called "tomboys". I usually ended up winning all the other boys' marbles, especially in the game called "Kraantjie". This is a game normally played on a sandy piece of ground. With a thin stick we marked an oval in the sand. Six marbles were placed in the Kraantjie. If three boys played, each would put two marbles in the pool. From a distance of 10 feet we would each get a chance to throw at one of the marbles in the oval. After a direct hit one got another chance to shoot. Most times I managed to win all the marbles in the pool. Thus I became the champion marble player of District Six.

Other popular games we played were with a kite, top or *kennetjie* and my favourite, *bok-bok.*

The children of Caledon and neighbouring streets were always ready for a game of *bok-bok*. Fourteen children, girls and boys mixed, could play. Each team consisted of seven members. A coin determined who started. One member of the fielding team, preferably the lightest in weight, was the "cushion". The rest of the team would bend their heads and interlock in a straight line as in a rugby scrum. The opposite team would stand in a long line. Each member would get a chance to jump on to the back of the fielding team. I would walk backwards, gather speed and run as fast as I could,

Playing Kerrim — Photo: Cloete Breytenbach

because the faster one ran the further one could jump. I would aim to land on the back of the first field member. The other six members then had a go. The fielding team had to stand firm. If one member collapsed, the game had to start all over again.

The first team member who jumped shouted *"Bok-bok, hoeveel op die rug?"* (Buck-buck, how many on your back?) The "cushion" (the member whose back was against the wall) was the witness when a number of fingers were held up by the member who jumped. If the answer was wrong, the game would start over.

Any number of children could play Blue Bottle. One child stands very still in the middle of the street with their head tucked in and, running at some speed, the next player jumps over the head of that child. The runner had to place both hands on the shoulders and jump over the child. This was a dangerous game. If the standing child moved it could be disastrous – but luckily for us we never got hurt!

All the games we played in the streets of District Six were great fun and a wonderful form of exercise. We were fit, happy and healthy. When we were not playing in the streets, we would go to the swimming-baths in Trafalgar Park. A whole day there cost just a tickey.

FIGHTING AT SCHOOL

Socially we were divided into two groups in standard five. Sait Petersen was the leader of my group and Bernard was the leader of the second group. The boys in Bernard's group called us "moffies", in other words boys who were not prepared to fight. They did this to provoke us. My main opponent was Abdullah Adams (Doellie). Doellie challenged me to a fight. After our fight, I arrived home with my shirt dirty and torn. My mother gave me a beating for fighting in the street. That was not the end of my punishment. When I got to school the following morning I was summoned to the principal's office and found Doellie was there too. Both of us got six of the best.

During playtime, Doellie's friends challenged me to a final fight. I did not want to fight again. I said no! But they called me all kinds of names. I plucked up courage and decided to accept the challenge. After school the two groups met on a field on the corner of Horstley and Constitution Streets. This time I removed my shirt. My heart was pounding but I told myself that I had to win. I grabbed Doellie when the fight started and threw him on the ground. Then I sat on top of him and punched with all my power. Bernard stopped the fight when Doellie's nose started bleeding. My friends held up my hands shouting that I was the winner.

The next morning on my way to school I saw Doellie standing on Plymouth Road corner. I wondered what his plans were. When I reached him, he took my hand and said I was "the champ". As we walked to school I told him I did not want to fight but I constantly received messages that he wanted to fight me. He said he had heard exactly the same about me. We agreed that it was our friends who were the trouble-makers. Since then, we have been the best of friends.

FIRST PAIR OF LONG PANTS

All through primary school, winter or summer, I had to wear short pants. This was the school uniform. It was only when I turned 13 that I was given my first pair of long pants. They were black Rustler jeans. My father had to decide when the time was right for me to wear long pants. When I turned 13, I told my father that I felt the time had come. About two weeks later, he told my mother that I was old enough to wear long pants.

One Saturday morning that summer she presented me with my jeans. What excitement! They were a bit long but I turned up the bottoms. I looked in the mirror and really liked the way I looked. I decided I had to venture outside and face the world. The big moment had arrived! But it took me nearly an hour to pluck up enough courage to leave the house. I knew that my friends, some in long pants and some in short pants, were going to tease me. They gathered around me outside our house in Caledon Street, inspecting me up and down, and made comments like, "Now you are a man." I strutted proudly all day with my hands in my pockets, enjoying a new feeling of confidence, but when my father saw me, he said "Take your hands out of your pockets when you are in the company of grownups!"

ISGAAK'S ACCIDENT

My mother sent Isgaak to the shop directly opposite Mr Parker's to buy some butter. Isgaak was six years old at the time. My father, who was looking through an upstairs window, watched him entering the shop and coming out with the butter. As Isgaak ran out of the shop, a van that was travelling at about 40 miles per hour, knocked him down. There was a terrible noise and we ran out of the house. My uncle Ismail just happened to be in the area. He was extremely upset. He approached the driver of the van and shouted at him angrily. A few moments later, my father was at the scene. Isgaak was lying on the ground bleeding. My father placed him in our car and rushed him to Woodstock Hospital. My brother Hoosain, cousin Yusuf Abrahams and I decided to follow them. We went to the emergency section where we found my father. He took us to a ward where the nurses were tending my brother. I touched Isgaak's hand and found he was still clutching the butter in his hand. He had a

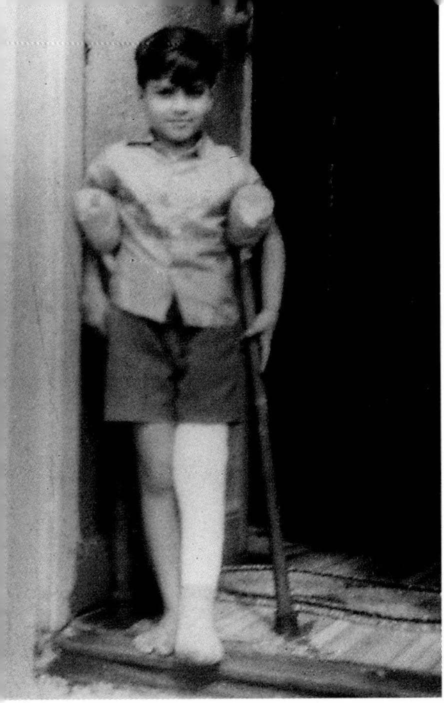

Isgaak's accident, photo taken in backyard of 247 Caledon Street

broken leg and a few bruises. He came home after six weeks but his leg was in plaster for a long time after that. During this time the man who was responsible for the accident never enquired about Isgaak.

After six months, Isgaak was back to normal but after that, whenever he had to cross the road, he was extra cautious.

SPORTS

All sports were learned in the streets of District Six. Soccer, cricket and rugby were the most popular. From standard four I played soccer for Ashley High Primary School. I also participated in gymnastics and athletics. I ran 100 metres relay as well as 400 metres. Our sports outfit was in green and gold, Springbok colours. Our school always took first prize in inter-primary school sports and athletic competitions. We competed against St Paul's, East Park (the Chapel Street School), St Marks, Trafalgar Junior and Gordon Primary School.

Because we always won, there was a rumour that the principal used ex-pupils for the main athletic events. This was not true. We were just very fit. Mr Brown was the PT instructor and we attended classes every Wednesday. We wore white shorts, shirt, socks and takkies (sandshoes). If we were not wearing the complete uniform, we were not allowed to attend the exercise class. Music was played during the class and, as soon as local housewives heard it start up, they gathered around the school fence with their small children to watch us.

Cricket

When I left school at the age of 15, I joined the Silvertree Club. I was the youngest player selected for the first team. I played for them for three years. Our first team was coached by the famous Tiny Abed of Aspeling Street.

Yorkshire Lads Cricket Team

Hoosain, Gabeba and Noor

DUTIES

My three sisters Gowah, Gabeba and Mariam, my brother Hoosain and I had to take turns washing the dishes. The girls' arrangement was that one would wash, one would dry and one pack away and sweep the kitchen. (Gowah was sometimes lazy and she would pay me a penny to do her share of the work).

Hoosain and I also had other duties. We had to scrub the three upstairs bedroom floors, the spiral staircase, dining-room, passage and kitchen floor. In addition I had to put Cobra white wax floor polish on the floors and rub them to a bright shine. This whole procedure would take me three hours. I had to do it every Friday until I was 15 years old.

On Saturday mornings, my mother would give me a list of

meat I had to buy from Mia's Butcher on the corner of Hanover and Horstley Streets. There were times when the shop was so full that I had to wait up to two hours to be served. The butcher first served adults and when I was eventually served I usually paid with money sticky with sweat from being tightly clutched for so long. After returning home, I was usually sent to buy groceries from Boeta Dulla Khan's shop opposite the Seven Steps in Hanover Street.

When Gowah was a teenager, she got a casual job at Boeta Dulla Khan's shop. He was very fond of her because she was a hard worker and he could trust her with money. The regular customers also liked Gowah as she was very quick.

My special Saturday afternoon treat was going to the Star Bioscope. I received one shilling pocket money for the matinee show. During interval I used to run to Mustaphar Fisheries in Hanover Street to buy half a loaf of bread and fish and chips. I even had change to buy a few sweets. I usually enjoyed this fish *"dite"* with ginger-beer in the bioscope.

TEENAGERS

On Sunday mornings the whole neighbourhood would come out of their homes when they heard the sound of Saint Mark's Brigade. The drum majorette twirled her baton impressively while parading a short distance ahead of the brigade. They played drums, trumpets, flutes and concertinas and they were always dressed in navy-blue uniforms.

The children in the brigade came from St Mark's Primary School. Even if we were in our pyjamas, we would run out of

Noor and Yusuf Kay in front of Movie Snaps in Darling Street

our house and accompany them to St Mark's Church. Sometimes we went into the church but mostly we played outside, waiting for the brigade to come out. I would play for a while and then run home after collecting koeksisters from the Jeppe family at number 9 Lewis Street. Once home I would make coffee and serve my parents in bed. This was our Sunday morning ritual.

After the service the brigade paraded through the streets of District Six. Sometimes I joined the crowd and marched alongside the band. I had to be home before afternoon prayers, however, to prepare for mosque. After prayers, I would go home for Sunday lunch. Family and friends would usually join us. Shortly after lunch we bathed and dressed in our Sunday best. On most Sunday afternoons I would meet my friends, Yusuf Abrahams of Ayre Street, Sedick Heneker of Caledon Street and Rashaad (Popeye) Isaacs of Stuckeris Street, and we would take a long and meandering route to the gardens off Government Avenue. We would stroll down Caledon Street, turn into Tennant Street then left into Upper Darling Street, left again at Adderley Street, finally move up Government Avenue and into the gardens. We would linger in the gardens to "tune" the girls. Sometimes we managed to befriend them but at other times they would shun us. (Now that I come to think of it, the girls were probably in the gardens for the same reason!)

If we succeeded in making the acquaintance of a girl, each of us would move away to talk to our new "girlfriends". Most of the girls were from the Bo-Kaap or from District Six. I always had to be home before dark so when it started getting that way, we would walk the girls to their homes. The girl who lived the furthest was taken home first. If the girls and boys liked each other they would plan to meet in the gardens the following Sunday.

Phone Booth, Stuckeris Street

PHONE BOOTH

Next to the public wash-house was a red telephone booth. The phone booth was popularly known as the "tickey box" as it cost a tickey ($2\frac{1}{2}$ cents) to make a call. The other phone booth was in Stuckeris Street. When we did not have a tickey, we took an open hairpin, placed one end in the receiver and, with the other end, scratched on the steel. Then we could talk endlessly without paying a cent. Only a handful of people knew this trick.

The tickey box was very important to me. When my girlfriends phoned me at home I was not allowed to speak for more than two minutes. On the odd occasion when I was allowed to phone, I was allowed to speak for two minutes only. Also, when my parents were present I was not comfortable speaking on the phone. When called to the phone I would say, "I'll call you back in five minutes" and then fly down the road to the phone booth next to the Westminister Cafe.

Sometimes in my excitement I forgot to take a hairpin with me. As soon as I realised this I would stop the first lady who passed by and ask for a hairpin. Then I could make the call and have a conversation for as long as I wished.

Whenever my mother noticed that I was missing, she would ask my brothers, "Where is Mogamad Noor?" They would say, "Mammie, after he got a phone call, he ran out of the house." Then she knew exactly where I was.

TRIMMERY (Trimmings)

Whenever we knew there was going to be a wedding, five friends, Yagja, Ismail, Yusuf, Ishsaam and Karriem, and I would offer to "trim" the room where the bachelor party was going to be held. The party was normally held on the Saturday night before the wedding on the Sunday.

All the furniture from the *voorkamer* (front room or lounge) was removed and placed in the back rooms and sometimes at the next-door neighbour's house. Crinkle paper of all colours was twisted into fancy patterns. This was hung from wall to wall, sometimes with balloons in the centre.

Friends of the future bride were invited and we danced to the music of Elvis Presley, Cliff Richard, the Shadows, the Platters and the Beatles. My favourites were "Summer Place" and "This Boy" by the Beatles. We would plan ahead which girl we were going to dance with, especially when we knew there was going to be a long-playing blues record on the Pilot gramophone and that the lights would be dimmed. The ladies of the house would serve refreshments like cold-drinks, usually Coke and Bashew ginger-beer, with cake. At about midnight, the six of us would stroll hand-in-hand with our partners while we walked them home.

The following day at the wedding we would be *bedienders* (waiters). We would meet at my house to dress in black suits, white shirts, black bow-ties, black shoes and white socks. At the wedding, trestle-tables would be laden with cakes, sweets, fruit, flowers and fancy biscuits. At suppertime we served roast chicken, potatoes, *soutvleis* (corned meat), home-baked bread and butter and salads. If there was a girl I liked, I would serve her the best of everything in the hope that I could walk her home and make a date with her.

We kept the guests entertained by singing "Rosa", "Forever and Ever", "Wedding Bells are Ringing", "They Try To Tell Us We Are Too Young", "Moon River", the famous Danny Williams song "Sixteen Candles", "Oh Carol" and "Breaking Up is Hard to Do".

Gowah (left) at 3 years and Mariam at 5 years in flower-girl dress at the Orange Leaf Cutting Festival.
Photo: Van Kalke, 1953

Noor   Dickman's Bakery, Caledon Street

DICKMAN'S BAKERY – OPPOSITE THE BRITISH BIOSCOPE

Up to about the age of 15 it was my job to buy fresh hot bread at Dickmans. My family's favourite loaf was called a floor loaf. It was not shaped like a normal loaf with a flat smooth top crust. The floor loaf had two ridges on top. It was creamy white and, when it was cut, the slices had a pretty pattern. The bakery also sold bread rolls and cakes for which people would queue. The people in District Six were fortunate because fresh bread, fish, fruit and vegetables were always readily available. Fresh produce was bought as it was required. Bread for our lunches was bought very early in the morning and the majority of school children and people who went to work took fresh sandwiches with them.

CALEDON STREET – CASSIEM'S BUTCHERY

Everybody in District Six went to Cassiem's Butchery for the best penny polonies. Having bought penny polonies, my friends and I would buy mango atchar from the corner shop or from Boeta Dulla Khan next to the Taj Restaurant in Hanover Street. We would take our purchases home, cut the polony in half lengthwise and fill it with the mango atchar. This delicious snack was then called "atchar dite". It was available at most of the Babbie shops for tuppence . A variety of this snack was the "chilli dite" penny polony filled with chillie, costing one and a half pennies.

Caledon Street

NEW YEAR'S EVE

New Year's Eve was the best day of the year. People did not go to sleep that night. They would walk the streets, wishing each other a happy New Year and the celebrations always lasted until the second of January. The Malay choirs sang Dutch *liedjies* as they paraded our streets. I was a member of a Malay choir.

The highlight of the New Year festivities was the Coon Carnival. People would place their benches along the shop fronts under the balconies in Hanover and Caledon Streets on New Year's Eve. Even my mother's favourite armchair was taken along so that she could watch the carnival in comfort. Visitors came from all over the Cape to District Six to watch the carnival.

People came for the New Year's Eve celebrations as soon as the shops closed. For two days and three nights they moved into well-placed doorways with their chairs and benches, mattresses and primus stoves. From here they would cheer on the Coons and Malay choirs as they paraded through Hanover Street. Often people rushed out to dance and romp around with the Coons as they passed. District Six was definitely the place to be on New Year's Eve.

COON CARNIVAL

I always wanted to be a singer. I longed to join the Coons, but my father refused to let me. At the age of 15, Yusuf Abrahams, Ishsaam Narker, Rashaad Kalie and I joined the Vikings Malay Choir. The club was in the Bo-Kaap. We had to attend meetings and practices three times a week. On one occasion, we participated in a major competition. Our choir leader said that one of us had to dress up as a woman for the "*moppie*" (comic song). Yusuf Abrahams volunteered. On the

2nd New Year, Coons, Caledon Street

Photo: Cloete Breytenbach
(District Six Collection)

night of the competition, we first performed as a combined chorus. After this came the *moppie* and Yusuf had to appear next to the lead singer. The song included words like, *"Toe vat ek om haar nekkie en soen haar in haar bekkie."* (So I placed my arms around her neck and kissed her on her lips). At this stage the lead singer had to take "her" in his arms and kiss "her" on the mouth. The audience roared with laughter and the people shouted, "Boeta Sulaiman, that's your son dressed as a woman!" They teased Boeta Sulaiman so much that he became upset. He had not, in the first place, approved of the idea that his son dress like a woman. We were very happy, however, as that night our team won second prize!

At the end of 1960, the Vikings disbanded and at the end of 1961, I said to a few friends, "Come, let's join the Coons." The next year, without our parents' knowledge, we joined "The Young Stars" Coon troupe. We attended practices on Sunday afternoons in the Cane Store in Martin Street. I fetched my uniform from the clubhouse in Ellesmere Street the day before New Year. I put it in a brown carrier bag and asked our neighbour to keep it for me until New Year's morning. I told Sis Gawa about my plans and she agreed to keep my secret. I knew that I could trust her. The next morning, I told my mother that I was spending the day with friends and went to collect my uniform. I changed in the clubhouse, painted my face with black and white cream and placed the yellow hat on my head. I was really pleased with the result. In front of the small mirror that was too high, I preened in the red, white and blue satin outfit with a yellow bow-tie!

When all the members were ready, we went to Boeta Sakkie's house in Aspeling Street. I walked via Caledon Street, right past my house, singing all the way. I was laughing up my sleeve, knowing that nobody would recognise me, yet knowing that if by any chance my father

College Boys Malay Choir

saw me, he would pull me out of the group, drag me home and give me a thorough scolding for disobeying him.

From Boeta Sakkie's house we went to the Green Point track. Here we took part in the singing competition and at 6pm we paraded back through Cape Town and through the streets of District Six. The same programme was followed on *Tweede Nuwe Jaar* (Second New Year). The following Saturday the finals took place and trophies were awarded to the winning teams. That year, "The Young Stars" took the first prize in ten categories! The only second prize we received was for "Best Dressed" because our yellow bow-tie and hat did not match our outfit. The first prize went instead to "The Hollywoods" whose colours were chocolate brown, light brown and white. The owner of "The Hollywoods" was Armani and his team also won a few prizes. After the prize giving, the Coon teams once again paraded through the streets and we showed off our trophies, carrying them high above our heads. The crowds cheered. I felt very proud of my team. We ended our parade with the singing of our last song "Exodus" with Joey Gabriels, the man who was known in District Six as South Africa's Mario Lanza. Later Joey Gabriels was to progress from the streets of District Six to sing at La Scala and the Metropolitan Opera House.

After our last song we paraded back to the clubhouse to change into our normal clothes. I left my hat there and rolled my Coon uniform and my Zorro's ("takkies" or shoes) into a small bundle.

I walked up Hanover Street. People were staring at me. I checked my fly. As I continued my way home people kept staring and commenting with shocked expressions. "Can it be? Mogamad Noor? Is it possible?" People were giggling and laughing at me as far as Horsburg Lane. I could not fathom it. Full of confidence I entered our backyard and closed the gate. As I turned around to enter the kitchen I came face to face with my father. He jumped up and grabbed hold of me shouting, "You bloody … So you have been with the Coons all day!" He was the angriest man alive at that moment. I was dumbfounded. "How does he know that I marched with the Coons? Who told him? Nobody except the members of my team know," I thought while he raged on, and I was convinced it was not one of them or Sis Gawa. How was it possible? My father lashed out at me and then shouted, "Look at your blerry face!" – I had forgotten to wash off the black and white cream!

STARLIGHT GANG

Every Friday and Saturday night, the Starlight Gang assembled on the corner of Caledon and Horsburg Lane, right outside our home. There they smoked "dagga" (marijuana) and cigarettes and, when the mood was right, they would sing. Their songs were often hits by the Platters, the Crew Cuts, the Aimes Brothers and the American Crooners. As a young man I enjoyed their singing and was inspired to become a singer. From time to time a fistfight would start with another gang over a girl or a disagreement. I enjoyed watching these. There were times when the fighting moved through the streets and the residents would follow the crowd to see which gang was winning.

Gangsters Photo: George Hallett

ROELAND STREET PRISON

The police were strict. When gangsters gambled on street corners, the police would suddenly appear. The gamblers would scatter in all directions. A policeman would pick up the money and dice and pocket them. If a gambler was unfortunate enough to get caught, the policeman would grab him by the collar and throw him into the back of a police van. The gambler would be taken to Caledon Square police station and was usually sent to the Roeland Street jail. The same thing happened to drunkards who were caught fighting in the streets.

I remember as a young boy accompanying a couple of gangsters who were taking food to friends in jail. This occurred on Sundays only. Their families packed curry and rice, roast meat, potatoes and vegetables into nice bowls. Sometimes there was also cake and fruit.

At the prison door the food was handed to a policeman who placed it in a prisoner's *blik bord* (enamel plate). However, when the prisoner was released, he would complain that he had had very little to eat. His family would tell him that they had sent very nice food on Sundays but he had obviously not received it.

On another occasion I went with my Uncle Ismail who took a loaf of bread to a friend. He sliced the bread lengthways, took out the inside, slipped in a packet of ten Cavalla cigarettes and some slices of polony and closed it. He wrapped it in plastic and gave it to the policeman.

Once when I waited outside the prison I peeped through a slit in the door and noticed where the food was placed. On a side wall there were small shelves which had prisoners' names tacked to them, but this was no guarantee that the food was handed over.

On Saturday or Sunday afternoons when my friends and I

walked past the prison, I saw prisoners working in the garden. They wore khaki shorts and short-sleeved shirts and were bare-footed in winter and summer. They had to work long hours and if they complained or if they were caught loafing, the policeman on duty would beat them with his baton.

THE HAWKERS

If a policeman found that a hawker did not have a licence, he had the power to confiscate his goods. The hawker was dragged off to prison, although sometimes he managed to escape capture. His green wooden wagon would be abandoned on the street. The policeman might help himself to some of the contents or take the wagon to the police station by tying it to the police van. Sometimes the wagon would topple over, scattering fruit and vegetables over the

Sheppard Street, daily fishmongers (horn constructed from a paraffin tin)

street and children in the vicinity would help themselves. If the hawker wanted his wagon back, he had to go to the police station and pay a fine of about a pound.

THE BURGLARY AT BANKS

The Star Bioscope was on the corner of Clifton and Hanover Streets. Next-door was Roger's Café, then came Star Furniture, the Star Bioscope Lane and then Banks. In the early 1960s Banks also acquired a shop next to the fish market. Next-door was a short lane leading into Vogelgezang Street where there was a storeroom. A big sign was painted on the building announcing BANKS HIRING SUPPLY.

Late one Friday night in 1963 I was on my way to fetch two friends, Hima (Ebrahim) and Faldie Dollie, who lived in Tyne Street and worked with me at the *Cape Times* where I had a casual job inserting the magazine section into the newspaper. Normally I walked down Horsburg Lane into

Hanover Street, 1970

Hanover Street, but on this night I happened to be in Clifton Street. The area around the fish market was full of people. As I got closer I saw men hurrying across Hanover Street carrying pots, pans, cutlery, bowls and crockery. A woman shouted, *"Hulle steel die winkel bankrot!"* (they are stealing the shop bankrupt). Someone at the back of the crowd shouted, *"Hey, hier kommie law!"* (Here comes the law).

At that moment, people streamed out of the Star Bioscope. The police, unaware of the burglary, were slowly cruising past. When the coast was clear, the thieves came out of hiding and continued with the burglary. They started handing out stolen goods and people hurried away with arms full of pots, pans and kettles. Some refused the stolen property, saying they did not want to end up in jail. The following day in the Star Bioscope, some people bragged about their new pots, pans and crockery, saying that they could now invite royalty to eat with them!

READER'S DIGEST

After I left school in the 1950s, the ginger-beer factory closed down and my father started his own business as a soft-goods dealer. He sold clothing, blankets, bed linen, tablecloths, dish cloths and towels. During the first few months, the business went well. As the months went by, however, it started to decline. His customers were poor payers and, before long, we were poor. My father was the only breadwinner and soon our electricity was cut off.

Gabeba (my eldest sister) and I decided we would give up going to school and get work to add to the family income. Our parents were against this plan but I could not bear seeing my mother struggle so hard. My eldest brother was an art student at the University of Cape Town and this influenced our decision. I managed to get a job at the

Reader's Digest where I started on 10th February 1961. Gabeba was employed at a clothing factory (Metro Clothing) in Roeland Street. Luckily we were able to walk to work and brought our wage packets to our mother unopened. We earned two pounds each per week.

Gabeba and I enjoyed our jobs. I was 15 years old and worked as a messenger. The Reader's Digest had no delivery vehicle. My co-worker, Denzil Clayton, and I had to wheel a basket four feet high from the office on the corner of Adderley and Church Streets to the main post office in Parliament Street, Cape Town. The basket was filled with long-playing records and books. When it had been emptied we wheeled the huge basket to another department of the Post Office to collect the post. Come rain or shine, we pushed that basket back and forth for almost a year.

When, in 1962, the Reader's Digest moved to the Parkade Building in Strand Street, a van was used for deliveries. It became my duty to take money to the bank. It was put into a strong brown leather bag which was locked and chained to my arm. I was escorted to the bank by Mrs Ford and Donald Nickles.

At the Readers' Digest, I had to wear a white shirt, navy suit and tie, black socks and shoes, and a navy cap with their badge on it. We were not allowed to wear coloured shirts. If we did, we were sent home to change. They paid for the uniform but we had to buy our own shoes.

During our lunch hour my friends and I met at a record shop in Regis House in Adderley Street. We listened to music of the Beatles, Neil Sedaka, Cliff Richard and Elvis Presley. I was known as "Joey" and for running errands I usually received cash tips from Tessa Reeves (she was in charge of the four messengers – Denzil Clayton, Peter Isaacs, Mogamat Benjamin and myself), Sheila Fraser and Mrs Welsch. Tessa's husband John Reeves was a broadcaster on the SABC

Pushing the trolley back to work, Movie Snaps, Darling Street, 1961

Movie Snaps, 1961

English radio. In 1963 John Reeves asked my brothers, four friends and myself to sing a traditional Nederlandse *liedjie* on radio. We sang "Rosa", which is traditionally sung at weddings.

My work chronology:

10th February 1961 – messenger

7th September 1965 – Roneo operator

7th May 1968 – assistant machine operator

20th November 1970 – machine operator

5th November 1974 – heat transfer operator

1975 – stock control clerk, supervising machine room, despatching, checking.

1985 – promoted to warehouse foreman with a staff of 40 workers.

I resigned on l July 1986.

I received several gifts from the Reader,s Digest on various anniversaries; 10th – a gold ring; 15th - super-eight projector; 20th – money; 25th – money.

Meeting the girls at lunchtime, 1961

Zerena Ebrahim, my daugher-in-law is carrying on the tradition as she is now employed by the Reader's Digest.

Today, Gabeba and I feel no regrets that we left school at such a young age. Due to our efforts, Hoosain became a commercial artist, Isgaak became a lecturer in mathematics as well as a draughtsman; Mariam became a nurse and then the matron of a hospital and now specialises in private nursing.

MARRIAGE

Galema and I married in 1964 in the Harvey Street Mosque. We moved into the house at 247 Caledon Street, which we shared with my parents, sisters and brothers.

The storage room that had housed the ginger-beer ingredients was cleared, cleaned and painted to become our room. The room was twelve by ten feet and had a big window facing the street, a high ceiling and solid wooden floors. Our bedroom suite consisted of a lady's wardrobe, a gent's wardrobe, a dressing-table with a stool and three mirrors, our bed, headboard and mattress. The furniture, made of imbuia, was bought at Van der Merwe's Furniture Store, Victoria Road, Woodstock, opposite the Gem Bioscope. I paid it off at R20 per month.

MY CARS

I married in 1964 when I was 20 and bought my first car, a red, two-door Hillman Husky for a hundred rand. I bought it from my Uncle Rashaad who lived in Princess Street, Walmer Estate. Petrol was then twenty cents a gallon. I kept the car for two years, sold it and bought a white 1964 Volkswagen Beetle. Since then I have owned Mercedes, Peugeot and Toyota cars.

GOWAH GETS ENGAGED

Gowah and Isgaak knew each other for quiet a while. They discussed their future with each other but they both needed their parents' blessing before embarking on any plans of their own. They had to follow the traditional route when they knew they wanted to get married.

First the engagement had to be arranged. Isgaak approached his parents and expressed his wish to ask Gowah Ebrahim of Caledon Street for her hand in marriage. His father asked his eldest brother to go to Gasant, my father, to inform him of this.

Once a suitable time and date was agreed, my mother and sisters set up a tea table in our front room. Gowah did not have to do anything except dress herself and be prepared for her engagement. When the time finally arrived, the uncle and his delegation came to the house. My whole family was in the room to greet the guests, except Gowah, who was anxiously waiting in the bedroom while her future was being planned.

The families greeted each other and the uncle spoke on behalf of Isgaak. He addressed my father saying," I am here on behalf of my brother's son Isgaak. He has sent me here to ask if he may marry your daughter Gowah." After listening to the uncle my father replied that he and my mother had no objection to this. They gave this marriage their blessing but said that the final word had to come from Gowah. My father called to Gowah, inviting her to join us. He said," Gowah come and stand here with your Mammie and me." She did as she was told and then my father told her that Isgaak had sent his uncle to ask if he could marry her. Gowah looked at all of us and then at my parents and said, "With the blessing of Daddy and Mammie I will marry him." She then looked at Uncle and said, "You can tell him that the answer is yes."

Uncle smiled broadly, reached into his pocket and took out a small red velvet box. He opened it and took out a beautiful engagement ring, which he placed on her finger.

The family gathered around Gowah and the uncle said a short prayer. The tea was served and just before the uncle left my father asked him to convey his best wishes to Isgaak's family and asked that they all get together to set a date for the wedding. About an hour later Isgaak came over to our house and we all congratulated him on his engagement. The excited couple then went over to Isgaak's house to continue the celebrations.

GOWAH GETS MARRIED

On the Sunday before Gowah's wedding we helped to put three trestle-tables in the front room and she placed freshly laundered tablecloths on them. Our house became a hive of activity. There was lots of excitement as family, neighbours and visitors swarmed about making biscuits and koeksisters and tea for all the visitors.

Visitors, neighbours and family members brought gifts all through the week. There were ladies who came to iron all Gowah's new clothes and her negligee sets.

As they completed the ironing of the garments they would hang them on decorated hangers from the picture frames for all to see. All her new shoes and slippers were arranged on the floor under the trestle-tables.

Gowah received gifts ranging from tablecloths, sheets, pillow-cases, bedspreads, hand-made doilies and curtains, to crockery and cutlery. Someone even gave her a chamber-pot beautifully decorated with flowers.

As the gifts were brought in they were placed on the table for all to see. If someone noticed that there wasn't a toaster or an iron, they would provide it.

Gowah's and Isgaak's wedding, 1974, Claremont Gardens

One Saturday evening as we all sat around the supper table Gowah's eyes swept around the room. She could not believe that all the gifts were for her. "I am so lucky to have such a wonderful family," she declared, quite overwhelmed. Later she asked sadly, "I wonder what will happen when the people of District Six have to move? They have been so kind and we are such a close community."

"Gowah, don't worry yourself with these kind of thoughts, it's your wedding day tomorrow. Finish your supper and go to bed," Daddy replied smartly.

Early the next morning a few ladies came over to iron Gowah's wedding dress and help her to prepare herself for this grand occasion.

At the wedding I heard someone say, "I gave Isgaak and Gowah an alarm clock for their wedding gift and set the alarm for 2am. They will get such a fright when it goes off at that time of the morning!"

I never asked whether it did.

THE FAST (RAMADAAN)

In the summer months during the fast my father would get up at 3am to prepare our breakfast of bread or toast with butter and polony or cheese. When the breakfast was ready, he would wake our mother. My favourite food at that time of the morning was cream crackers (a dry water biscuit). When this was served, my father would shout from the kitchen "Cream crackers, cream crackers!" When I heard this I would jump out of bed and practically fly down the 18 steps to the kitchen. If my father did not shout "Cream crackers", I was not interested in eating. After breakfast, all of us would help clean the kitchen and my father would go to the Muir Street Mosque for morning prayers.

Hoosain, Isgaak and I would go to the mosque in Ellesmere Street because prayers at this mosque ended earlier than those at the Muir Street Mosque. As Muslims we were entitled to attend any mosque and my father did not object to this. At about 4.30am after prayers, the men walked back to their homes without being disturbed by anyone lurking about.

After our 3.45am breakfast, we would not eat again until 8pm. At 6pm mothers and daughters would start preparing the supper. Dishes included soup, curry and rice, breyani or bredies (stews) and also koeksisters, samoosas, daltjies (chilli bites) and pancakes.

After 7.30pm, the neighbours would send plates of delicacies to each other and at times our table was filled with 20 different kinds of cake. At five minutes to 8 all the children of the immediate neighbours, Muslim as well as non-Muslim children, would gather at the corner of our house to watch the lights at the top of the Muir Street Mosque come on. Then everyone would shout "*Wagtoe*!" (meaning "now is the time to break the fast"). The children would run back to their

Al-Azhar Mosque, Aspeling Street

homes. The streets of District Six would be empty and quiet, for while the Muslim people broke their fast children were kept indoors as a token of respect.

We broke our fast by eating a date or a samoosa and we drank a little soup or water. Immediately after this, the boys and men would walk briskly back to the mosque for additional prayers. These would not last too long and afterwards we practically ran home for the evening meal with the family. About half an hour after our meal, we went back to the mosque to say the last prayer of the day, including an additional special prayer called *"Taraweeg"*. This would last approximately an hour. This prayer was said especially during the fast.

Fasting lasted for 29 (sometimes 30) days. One week before the end of the fast, children would get excited as they knew they would be getting new clothes and shoes. My parents bought suit lengths from British Cloth, a fabric shop in Hanover Street. Our suits were made by Boeta Aghmat. He was a tailor who was also our neighbour. If they were not bought my sisters' dresses were made by Aunt Fatima, the dressmaker of Princess Street, Walmer Estate. During the 1950s it was traditional for all men and boys to wear a red fez. Occasionally someone would wear a black fez and these could be bought at Wayniks in Hanover Street.

After the fast a special day, Eid Ul Fitr (also known as Labarang) was celebrated. Between 8.30 and 9.30am we would dress in our new clothes and proceed to the mosque for special prayers. Afterwards we would greet our parents and sisters. Then we would walk along the streets of District Six to say *"Slamat"*, wishing one and all a happy Eid. The best part of the day for us was receiving money from people. We were also offered cakes, sweets and cooldrinks. After a celebration lunch at home we would walk to our families in Walmer Estate, Woodstock and Salt River to continue our season's greetings. Towards evening we would return home tired, with sore feet, because we all had new shoes, and with pockets full of pennies. Relieved to be back home my brothers and I would go to our rooms to count our money. My father would suddenly appear in the doorway and say, "You must keep some of the money for bread," and we willingly gave him a share.

DEATH

When somebody died in District Six, the *Malboet* (messenger who brought the sad news of a Muslim's death) let everybody know. Terry "Malboet" and Boeta Yusuf were two of these people. There were times when Terry could not advise every Muslim family about a death and the time and place of the funeral. He would knock on the door of the first house in a street and ask them to spread the word. He would state the time of the funeral and people would turn up one hour ahead of time. The women of the neighbourhood went even earlier to prepare food. They would make dishes like carrot or bean stew which were served with rice.

My Father Gasant

The body was wrapped in white linen and placed in a *katel* (bier). The men carried the body by foot from District Six to the cemetery in Observatory next to Groote Schuur Hospital. People with lorries and cars would transport the men back to the house of the deceased.

At the cemetery, we would pray for about half an hour. When the funeral was over, Terry would invite everyone present to the house of the deceased to have a meal. From the following night the whole neighbourhood, family and friends would come to the same house for seven consecutive nights to pray. On the seventh night after the funeral, the biggest gathering was held and cake and tea were offered. Each person took home a *Bakarat*, a brown paper bag filled with home-made cake and biscuits, oranges, bananas, apples and sweets.

After seven days, prayer meetings were held on Thursday nights up to the fortieth day after the death. On this day the men who attended the funeral would go to the cemetery to say final prayers for the deceased. Once more a gathering was held and food was served at the house of the deceased.

When a married Muslim man died his widow would have to stay indoors for four months and 10 days. If she had a job, she would continue going to work but she would have to stay indoors after work and on weekends. If she had nobody to do her shopping, she was allowed to do it, as well as perform other obligations.

BABBIE SHOPS

After 6pm during the week, Babbie shops (small cafés) were not allowed to sell groceries, paraffin, methylated spirits, sugar, tea, coffee or tinned food. If the police found that shopkeepers were selling any of these items, they would fine them. The only commodities that could be sold after this time were cigarettes, matches, cooldrinks, bread, sweets, chocolates, magazines, ice-creams and ice lollies (suckers). If the police caught the shopkeeper red-handed, they would "strike a deal", that is accept a bribe. The shopkeeper would give the police cigarettes and chocolates. There were many instances of police stopping their van outside the shop, when one policeman, usually the driver, would stay behind while the other would go inside. He would slap his hand on the counter and say, "Hey! Cool-drinks and cigarettes!" irrespective of whether the shopkeeper was serving a customer or not. Customers would stand quietly and not say a word until the police van drove away and then make comments like, "Who do they think they are coming into the shop and just demanding luxuries for free?"

THE CRESCENT RESTAURANT IN HANOVER STREET

This was the best restaurant in District Six. The owner was Mr A H Kathrada, known as "Katz". The interior was posh and the food excellent. Because of the apartheid laws the people of District Six were not allowed to eat in restaurants in Cape Town or Sea Point. When white people wanted to have a meal with non-white friends they would come to the Crescent. Many white people who worked in and around District Six came to the Crescent for lunch. Even Nelson Mandela met his friends at the Crescent when he was a young man. One of the delicacies of the Crescent was an Indian sweetmeat known as "pink jellybean".

Douts Café, Hanover Street

DOUTS CAFÉ

Douts Café was on the corner of Blythe and Hanover Streets. The best curry was sold here at one shilling and sixpence (15 cents) for a big plateful, so many families could afford to buy take-away curry. Gangsters often ate there.

WESTMINSTER CAFÉ

This café was close to the wash-house and next to British Cloth in Hanover Street. They made the grandest *dahltjies* and gangsters liked going there to eat, especially their meals of curry and rice or curry and roti.

MR LAING'S CHEAPSIDE CLOTHING STORE

Mr Laing's Cheapside Clothing Store was in upper Darling Street. One could buy clothes at this store and pay off two shillings and sixpence (25 cents) per week. Mr Laing went around to his customers on Friday nights to collect. He never knocked first, he just opened the front door. If the customer did not have money to pay him, he would shout, "F... you! See that you have my money next week!" He was never robbed while collecting his money in District Six.

We had a good relationship with Mr Laing. If he came to our house while we were having supper, he would pull out a chair, sit down and help himself to food. As teenagers, my friends and I usually dressed in similar trousers and shirts, especially on Sunday afternoons when we went to the gardens to meet our girlfriends. Whenever we needed new trousers and shirts, Mr Laing supplied us at a cheap price. That was why the store was known as Mr Laing's Cheapside Clothing Store.

DIE WASBADS (THE WASHBATHS)

The washbaths were situated in Clifton Street behind the fish market. A bar of soap could be bought for one penny, and one could hire a clean towel at very little cost. Each individual was allowed 15 minutes in a bath or shower cubicle. If one took one moment longer, the caretaker would bang on the door and shout, "Come, come, hurry up, we haven't got all day. The queue is very long. People can't sit here all day!"

The tradition in the men's section was for two people to sit back to back on the benches to await their turn but the gangsters did not follow this procedure. They would go directly to a shower and peep through a hole in the door to see if the person inside was dressing. Then the gangster would dash into the shower as soon as the occupant came out.

Many well-known singers, like Joey Gabriels and Salie "Uiwe" Daniels (one of the leads in the David Kramer and Taliep Petersen shows) practised their singing in the showers. There were also singers from the Platters, the Rockets, the Silhouettes and the Star Gazers. There was Solly Junior who sang like Engelbert Humperdinck, Rudolf Walker who sang like Nat King Cole, Dougie Schrikker who sounded like Frank Sinatra and Joey Gabriels whose voice reminded one of Mario Lanza. Many singers could imitate Elvis Presley and Cliff Richard.

The Washbaths, Clifton Street Photo: Fakier Jessa

The *moffies* (homosexuals) would go into the showers four or five at a time. They would be there for such a long time that the people on the benches would shout at them to come out. Les, one of the strongest of the *moffies* did not allow anyone to mess with him though, not even the gangsters.

The last time I went to the public baths was in 1974. I went to say goodbye to everyone. I told them, "I am leaving District Six and I don't know if I will ever see you again." In fact, I did not see them again for nearly 20 years. It was only after the District Six Museum was established that I met any of them again.

THE BIOSCOPES

The Star Bioscope

The Star bioscope was on the corner of Clifton and Hanover Streets. It held many variety shows and if a performer was worth his salt, the Star bioscope was a good place to be. The reaction of the audience determined the performer's future. If the act was not to their taste, they would hurl rotten tomatoes at the stage. Insults could be heard from all sides. One just had to get off that stage as soon as possible. One did not have to go to Hollywood for an audition, this advice was handed out free. There was a saying: "If you do not make it at the Star, you will never make it anywhere." But if the performance was good, then one's path was surely paved with gold. The audience would scream with joy, "Here's the next Nat King Cole!" or "... the next Frank Sinatra!"

The Star bioscope was a very special place. Many famous Cape Town artists performed there at one time or another. These included Joey Gabriels, the Rockets, the Platters, Zayn Adam, Taliep Petersen. Soon after District Six was declared a whites-only area, the Star biscope burned to the ground.

Patrons never had the patience to queue. They would push and shove their way to the ticket office. Children would scamper between patrons' legs and sneak into the bioscope unnoticed. Sometimes gangsters would push ahead of people and force their way in. Some gangs claimed their own seats. They carved their names on the backs of these seats and if someone dared sit on one of them they were quickly removed by gang members. If the offender was someone from another gang, a fight would break out in the bioscope. Normally it was accepted that one did not take one of these seats.

After the screening of a film, there would be heated discussions and arguments among the viewers. When the film "Madame X" was shown, the manager of the Star Bioscope handed out packets of tissues to the ladies, although several of the men shed a few tears as well.

Serials and favourite movies

There was something special about the serials which were shown on Saturday afteroons. "King of the Congo" with Buster Crabb was one of my favourites. So was the "Invisible Man" and "Batman and Robin". I often went to watch these serials and tried never to miss an episode.

Other movies we watched were "Jail House Rock" and "King Creole" starring Elvis Presley; "Summer Holiday" (Cliff Richard); "Where the Boys Are" (Connie Francis); and the cowboy films with Roy Rogers, Tex Ritter, Jimmy Wakeley and Charles Starret.

The National Cinema

This cinema was in William Street. It was originally built as an opera house. It had three floors and, when two floors were full, late-comers were accommodated on the steps of the gallery. Many gangsters preferred to sit there because they could smoke their dagga undisturbed. The only time I sat there was on an occasion when my girlfriend insisted on seeing Rock Hudson in "Farewell to Arms" and the cinema was full.

Many variety shows were held at the National Cinema. Zaakie Fredericks, one of my friends from Ashley High Primary School, took part in pantomimes and ballet classes and performed there from an early age. As he grew older he performed for many organisations, including old age homes and hospitals. Later Vincent Vee (Igshaan Veenendaal), Karriem Darries, Rusty Wilson and Ismail Isaacs joined him. They called themselves "Zaakie and Friends". They always performed free of charge because they loved music and

National Cinema

entertaining. Later this group was joined by Rashaad, Craig and Boeta. Many singers have been influenced by Zaakie's generosity. He died in the early 1990s.

The British Bioscope

The British Bioscope was on the corner of Caledon and Cannon Streets. Gangsters were always hanging out on its steps. On warm days gangsters would open the windows wide and light would stream in, straight on to the screen. Then, of course, the film could hardly be seen, and the patrons would scream for the windows to be closed.

The Avalon Cinema

The Avalon was on the corner of Hanover and Russell Streets. Here a guy was proud to take his girlfriend. Men were not allowed to enter the cinema without a jacket. Unsavoury characters were not allowed in and anyone caught smoking cigarettes in the cinema was immediately

Staff in front of the Avalon Cinema

thrown out. Children were not allowed to watch films at night. Younger ones went to matinees or the 5.30pm show. The best films were shown at the Avalon. The interior was luxurious and one could sit in comfort.

Manager Noor "Chat" Frieslaar was a strict but popular manager. After he died in the 1970s, people were concerned about his successor. Abduraghmaan (Maantjie) Jacobs was suggested. He was my friend and when I was working at Reader's Digest during the 1960s, I often met him during my lunch break. At that time he worked for the Public Works Department. Maantjie had five brothers, Sedick, Toyer, Salie, Yusuf and Omar, and they were known as the Bakkar Brothers. They were very tough guys, and Maantjie was the strongest. He was not afraid of gangsters and because he was always ready to help people, he was appointed as manager.

Maantjie soon became popular and attendance increased. People felt safe. Daja closed his barber shop opposite the Avalon and joined Maantjie as joint manager. Salama was the friendly cashier and if I took her home she would often invite me for a late supper. When they were busy I would help my cousin Gasant "Santjie" Abrahams at the door while she ushered people to their sets.

Banana Rama

Banana Rama was in Reform Street close to Chapel Street. Banned films were secretly shown there. The owners had two projectors. One was used to show the banned film while the other had a legal film just in case the law should check up. Outside the Banana store a "watchman" would be on guard to send a warning signal if the police showed up. It cost 50 cents to watch a banned movie and only adults were allowed in. People sat on wooden benches and chairs. The Banana Rama could seat 150 people.

THE FISH MARKET

The fish market was on the corner of Hanover and Clifton Streets, opposite the Star Bioscope. There were nine fish stalls. People came from all over the Cape to buy fish, especially on Monday mornings. Mondays were fish days, because the majority of people had roast meat or chicken for lunch on Sundays.

Each housewife had her favourite stall, as owners knew what their customers liked, be it fresh snoek, stockfish, crayfish, harders, masbankers, hottentot, red roman, white stumpnose, geelbek (yellowtail) or kabeljou. It was not a problem if cash was not available because fish was sold on "tick" (on account) and this was normally paid on the Friday evening of the same week. It was not necessary for people to go hungry. If money was scarce one could ask the stall owner for snoek *gratte* (snoek bones) or snoek heads which were given free of charge.

Easter was the busiest time at the fish market because it was a tradition in District Six to make pickled fish for Easter. Housewives would queue early in the morning on Thursday before Easter to buy the freshest selection of their favourite fish. The fish market was also the place where one could pick up the latest gossip.

When District Six was demolished, Cape Town lost something very special. The fish market was a landmark that now exists only in the memories of those who once knew it.

The Fish Market, Hanover Street Photo: Clarence Coulson

SOME PEOPLE FROM DISTRICT SIX

Sis Gawa and Poefie

Her speciality was making *konfyt* (watermelon preserve). When watermelons were in season, neighbours and her family would save the skins. Sis Gawa put them into a large tub to be washed. The children would help her to cut off the top hard green skin, leaving the soft section. This was pricked with a fork. We sat around a big wooden table while Sis Gawa told many stories. This went on for hours. Sometimes we listened to Springbok Radio's "Consider Your Verdict" and "The Creaking Door" or to their programmes of popular music. After soaking the rinds in lime (bought at Sperber's Chemist in Hanover Street), Sis Gawa washed them off, added dried ginger and cooked the mixture on a primus stove until the rinds were soft. Then sugar was slowly added. She supplied weddings and other functions with her *konfyt*. It was believed that Sis Gawa made the best *konfyt* in District Six.

When District Six was bulldozed, Sis Gawa's daughter Gadija, known as "Poefie", took a wheelbarrow, collected fallen bricks and sorted them in her backyard. We laughed at her, not understanding what was in her mind. Six months before they had to leave the area, we learned that their family used the bricks to build their house in Surrey Estate.

The Fighting Brothers

There were two sets of brothers constantly at each other's throats. Boy and Punte lived in Horsburg Lane and Kassiem and Achmat opposite my house in Caledon Street. Kassiem was a boxer and fought Boy, while Agmat tackled Punte. Each set of brothers had supporters. The crowd would cheer a good fight. Usually Kassiem landed the first punch on Boy and blood would flow. The fight would continue until the crowd felt that they had had enough. Before serious damage was done, the men would step in and stop the fighting. After this, the fighters would go home and clean up. Boy and Punte would stay indoors for the rest of the day to recover. The following day both sets of fighters would shake hands and be friends. But as soon as the peace was disturbed between these two sets of brothers, the crowds would reappear for another fight.

Sandra MacGregor

As a small child I often noticed a young woman painting in the streets of District Six. She painted scenes of the people, buildings and mountains. As children, we were fascinated by the magic she created on canvas. The gangsters never bothered her. They protected her and carried her painting equipment for her. They would sometimes even pose for her. They loved to do this.

Photo courtesy of Sandra MacGregor

During the school holidays we would wait for her to arrive and gather around her. We enjoyed being near her. She was, in our eyes, not only kind and friendly but beautiful. She was petite with long black hair. She encouraged us to take up painting. My brother Hoosain was so inspired by her he started to paint and, after he left school, studied art at the University of Cape Town.

In the evening, when she left District Six for home, her equipment would be carried by either the children or the gangsters to Majiet's house where it was stored. Majiet loved doing things for Sandra. As a young boy, he was one of her secret admirers. All the people loved her and kept her refreshed with food and tea sweetened with condensed milk, or on very hot days with cold drinks.

She came to District Six for many years. Sometimes newspaper photographers would record her and her young admirers. The kids would scream with excitement, "Did you see, we are in the newspaper!" However, it all came to an abrupt end when there was nothing left to paint of the old District Six.

Johaar Mosaval

Johaar Mosaval was born in District Six, at 1 Little Lesar Street, opposite the Seven Steps. He attended Muir Steet Primary until standard three. In 1932 he went into standard four at Ashley High Primary School, where he was one of their first pupils. At the age of 12 he took part in his first pantomime, "Beauty and the Beast". It was in this production that he was discovered by the director of the University of Cape Town ballet school, Dulcie Howes.

After being principal dancer in "Cinderella" in standard five and "Ali Baba" in standard six, Johaar was invited to be in a production of "The Tempest", performed in the Cape Town City Hall and choreographed by Dulcie Howes. From

1947 to 1949, he received three years of training at the University of Cape Town ballet school.

When the famous British dancer Anton Dolin came to South Africa to dance with Alicia Markova at the Alhambra Theatre, an audition was arranged for Johaar. Under normal circumstances, this could not have happened, as apartheid laws were at their height at that time, but through the influence of Dulcie Howes, an audition was arranged. Johaar's performance was so impressive that the press were

Johaar Mosaval, La Boutique Fantasque. Copyright: Anthony Crickmay
Photo courtesy of Johaar Mosaval

called in and a special fund for sending him to the Royal Ballet School in London was inaugurated. He left for London in January 1950 when he was 22 years old. At the Royal Ballet School, he passed his exams with honours. Dame Nanette de Valios arranged for him to join the Sadlers Wells Theatre Ballet, now known as the Royal Ballet, and within two weeks he was chosen for his first major role in the ballet "Pineapple Poll". In 1956, he became a soloist, and in 1965, a senior principal of the Royal Ballet.

Six days after the coronation of Queen Elizabeth in 1952, Johaar was chosen to dance his first solo. The production was "Gloriana", an opera specially composed for the occasion by Benjamin Britten. It was to be performed at the Royal Opera House, Covent Garden.

Johaar Mosaval has performed in all the major capitals of the world. He returned to South Africa in 1976, when he played the role of Petrouchka in the Nico Malan Opera House to thunderous applause and a standing ovation.

"Kafunta" Mogamat Benjamin

Mogamat was born in 1957 in Chapel Street and lived at 10 Mackenzie Street, District Six. He was the second-eldest child in a family of 11 children. He attended school at Albertus Street Primary and the School of Industry Primary Schoool.

Although he loved school, he had to leave when he was 12 years old due to financially strained circumstances at home. He got his first job as a general worker at a bookshop in Cape Town where he was paid a meagre wage. However, this was a great help to his family.

Mogamat missed school, especially Mrs Hartnick of Albertus Street School who, along with his mother, was his best friend. He started playing netball at the age of 10 years and it became his favourite sport. The first club he belonged to was the Silvertree Supremes and the second was the International Netball Team. He eventually became an umpire and sat in at board selections for the netball unions. He was umpire and convenor for the Mannenberg (on the Cape Flats) and Metropolitan Bonteheuwel Netball Unions. He also played a major role in coaching netball players for the Western Province Netball Association.

At one of the national games in Port Elizabeth in 1977, a woman team member broke her leg and Mogamat came to the rescue. Disguised as a woman, he played centre! Needless to say his team won the tournament.

Mogamat joined the Coon Carnival troupe Odds & Ends whose headquarters were in De Korte Street. One year he was the lead drum majorette. His outfit consisted of a long cream beaded lurex dress with slits for easy movement. The headgear was a fancy turban and he wore large gypsy earrings, lots of glitter and make-up. He loved performing and dancing to the beat of banjos, guitars and tambourines.

When District Six was demolished, Mogamat was moved to Lavender Hill but moved again to Bonteheuwel. He now works as the manager of a shop close to the District Six Museum. He feels that the atmosphere in the museum has helped him to overcome his anger. It reminds him of the past and those memories that are part of his mind, heart and body.

"So much has changed since I had to leave District Six. What I miss most is my home in McKenzie Street, its warm and welcoming atmosphere, summer with its gentle breeze from the sea close by. Winters meant warm soup and home-made bread smothered with butter. The kids of District Six would run out into the rain with bowls and plates to catch the hail, not caring about getting wet! I also loved the whirlwinds. Sometimes a whirlwind would appear and I would run into the centre and imagine that it would take me

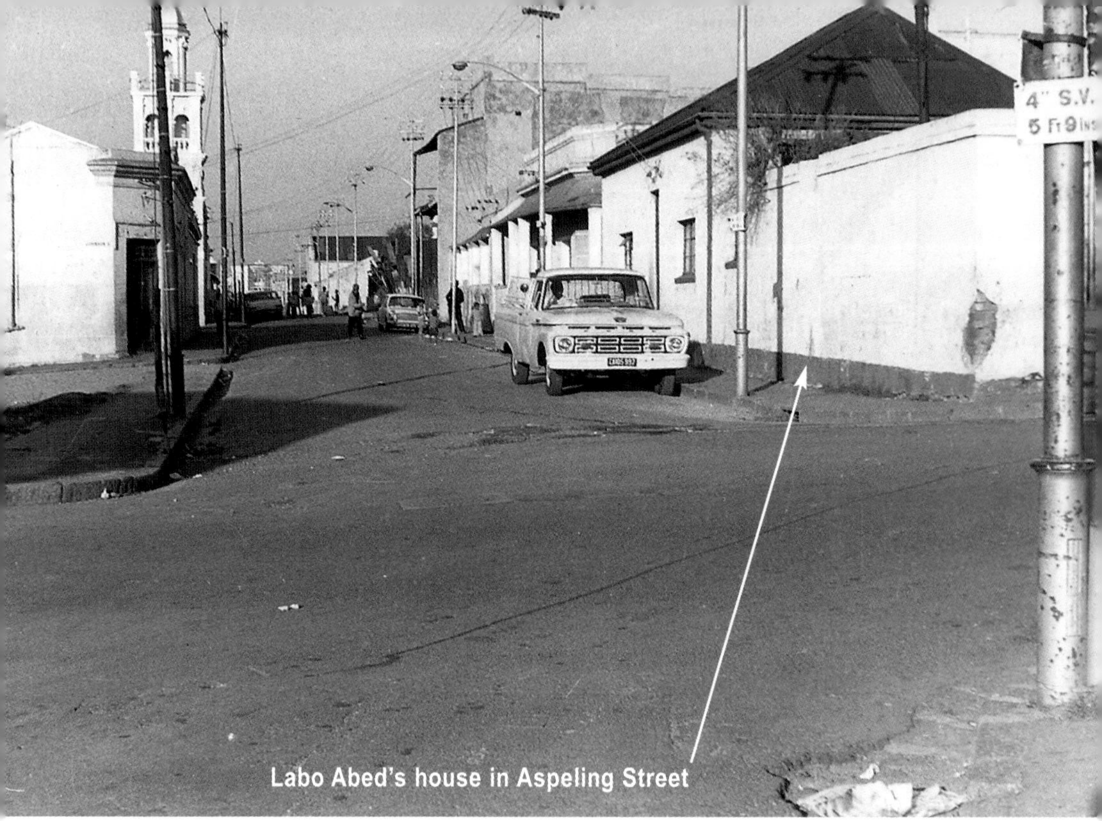

Labo Abed's house in Aspeling Street

up to heaven. I miss my neighbours, the Christmas choirs and church brigades and I hope that at some time in the future the Coon Carnival will again offer the entertainment and extravaganza that we so loved."

The Abeds

The Abeds were a well-known District Six family. They originally came from India and, after living in Durban, settled in Aspeling Street, District Six. There were five brothers: Abduraghman (Baboo), born in India in 1926; Gasant (Tiny), born in Durban in 1928; Salie (Lobo), born in Durban in 1929; Goolam (Goelie), born in Durban 1938 and Sulayman (Dik), born in Cape Town in 1939.

As a youngster I often watched the Abed brothers playing rugby and cricket in Aspeling Street. All the brothers became excellent sportsmen but, due to the apartheid laws, they never received the recognition they deserved. Opportunities in sport depended on the colour of one's skin.

"Coloured" sportsmen could play cricket and rugby for South Africa but only as "coloured" Springboks. "Coloured" sportsmen played for Western Province Union and not Western Province Rugby Board, which allowed "white" membership only.

My hero was Salie (Lobo). To my mind, he was the greatest wicket-keeper in South Africa and, as my hero, he was the best in the world! In 1997, Lobo visited the District Six Museum. He brought along his brother Goelie who was visiting Cape Town from England. Lobo gave me a short description of the sporting careers of his brothers.

Abduraghman (Baboo)

Baboo represented Western Province for 20 years, from the age of 19. He also played cricket for Roslyns, the District Six rugby and cricket club. He became an accredited rugby and cricket umpire and referee.

Gasant (Tiny)

Tiny played cricket for the Indian Union and was selected for Western Province in the Indian Tournament, where he scored a century. At that time he was 16 years old. Later he was selected for South Africa as vice captain on a cricket tour.

Gasant also played rugby for Roslyns and played for South Africa in two test matches. He became a regular cricket and rugby player for Western Province.

Salie (Lobo)

Lobo played rugby for Roslyns. In 1947 he was selected for Western Province, although not originally for the first team, but he scored a try and was promoted to the first team. From

1953, he concentrated on cricket. There is one cricket game I have never forgotten. This was when Lobo stumped a player. The batsman missed the ball and Lobo caught it. The batsman's foot was in the air and he was obviously out, but the umpire did not dismiss him. All Lobo's fans witnessed this and we were very unhappy about the decision.

Photo: Salie (Lobo) Abed

Goolam (Goelie)

Goelie represented Western Province as an all-rounder in a Johannesburg tournament. He moved to Roslyns and was unlucky not to make the Springbok side to Kenya. He went to England and played rugby for Northern Bradford for a few years and was very successful. Subsequently he played cricket in the Lancashire league as an all-rounder. On one occasion, when he was playing against Garfield Sobers who was bowling, Goelie hit three sixes. After the match Sobers went to the dressing-room to congratulate him on hitting those sixes.

Sulayman (Dik)

Dik never played rugby but became a good cricketer, playing

for Roslyns from the age of 15. He also represented Western Province at cricket and was captain several times. He went to England, where he played in the Lancashire league as a medium fast bowler and was considered a very good batsman. He left England and moved to Holland where he captained the national team. Eventually, he gave up cricket and settled in Holland.

While I was still wearing short pants, I visualised the Abed brothers as Springbok cricketers and as Springbok rugby players, but this was never to happen. Nevertheless, they are still remembered as District Six's best sportsmen.

DREAMS

In 1995 I had a dream that I was watching bulldozers at work in District Six from early in the morning until late at night. I observed how each and every house was being demolished. I parked my Beetle in front of my house. The homes next to mine, numbers 249 and 251 as well as 253, were being bulldozed by the metal monster. It was getting late. I was standing in front of my car. I heard one of the workers asking the foreman, "What about house number 247?" He replied, after looking at his watch, "It is almost six o'clock. Ag man, leave that one." I reached for my keys, got into the car and drove home. As I entered my house in Athlone, I shouted to my wife, "Galema, pack up, we are going back. The house is still standing!" I telephoned a friend to bring his lorry straight away. He asked me why and what the urgency was. I told him that I was going back to District Six. He replied, "Noor, it's not possible man, you must be dreaming. Did you forget that your house was bulldozed?" I told him not to argue and to hurry up. He soon arrived at my house in Athlone. We loaded the furniture and all our belongings on to the truck and when we reached my old house we unloaded and moved back into our old house. That night I had a wonderful sleep in my old home.

Another night I woke up in a sweat because I dreamt that I was the driver of a bulldozer and I was on my way to demolish the technikon which was built on the old sites of District Six. In fact, the land on which our house stood (it was next to St Mark's Church which still stands) now belongs to the technikon. When I got there, all the ex-residents had turned up to witness the destruction of the technikon.

TOWARDS AN ENDING

I lived for 17 years in Athlone and when my son Isgaak and Zerena married, they built a "granny flat" for my wife and myself on their property. We are now living with them in Rondebosch East. Galema looks after Muneer, Razeen and Ishtiyaq, our grandchildren.

Isgaak is a civil engineering technician and Mariam, my daughter, who is married, does administrative work.

As soon as it is official, my wife and I would like to return to live in District Six.

MY PIGEONS COME HOME

By 1975 I was fortunate enough to have saved sufficient money to buy myself a house in Athlone. This meant that I would not have to move to any of the areas designated for ex-residents of District Six, including Mitchells Plain, Hanover Park, Lavender Hill and Belhar.

So, on a warm day in January 1975, my wife and I with our two children, aged three and five, moved to our new home in Athlone. With our belongings were my prized racing pigeons, for whom I had built a loft, using the same wood that had made up the loft in District Six.

After three months in Athlone, I felt that it was time to let the pigeons fly free to see if they would return home. I was fully aware of the possibility that not all of the pigeons would return to their new home in Athlone. When I returned home that evening, the first thing I did was visit the loft. "Where are my pigeons?" I asked my wife. Not a single pigeon had come back.

After a sleepless night I returned to work the next morning, driving, as I always did, through the demolished landscape that was once District Six. As I drove past the now empty plot that used to be my home in Caledon Street, I saw a sight which shook me to my core: my pigeons, all 50 of them, were congregated on the empty plot where our home had stood. Getting out of my car, I walked over to where the pigeons were. Very surprisingly, they did not fly away, but looked into my eyes as if to ask: "Where is our home?"

EPILOGUE

The day I left our house in District Six, never to return, I knew that my life had changed forever. In bitterness and anger, I accepted what was inevitable. In this memoir, I tell my story and the story of my family, how we lived, what we cared about and how it all came to an end. We were ordinary people, living a rich and satisfying life. We cared for each other and about each other. And when it ended, I thought my happiness had received a blow from which it would never recover.

Who would have thought that, with the establishment of the District Six Museum, there would be a return of meaning into my life. The museum was established in 1992 as a two-week exhibition, to commemorate the destruction of District Six. Let me quote from our first newsletter: "In many ways,

Noor Ebrahim laid the foundation upon which this museum has been built. Some of the most recognisable and most frequently reproduced images of District Six were taken with the Voigtlander camera that he bought with his brother Hoosain."

This was just the start of exciting events which I could never have predicted. The museum has flourished from its inception. It has become a symbol of remembrance and survival in our country. The photographs and artefacts donated by ex-residents have become the nucleus of an on-going series of exhibitions. The museum has captured their loss for all to see.

Famous people from all over the world acknowledge the museum's importance, and we have welcomed their visits and tributes.

The first prominent person to come to the museum was United States Vice-President Al Gore, in December 1995. It was a significant visit and memorable for me. I showed him the exact location of my house on a floor map, and explained to him how many other people had suffered the same experience of dispossession, and how the face of District Six had changed forever.

Sandra Proselandis, Al Gore and Noor, at the District Six Museum on 6 December 1995

Noor with Mary Robinson at the District Six Museum on 26 March 1996

Not long after, in came Mrs Mary Robinson, President of Ireland and a former student of our then Minister for Water Affairs, Kader Asmal, who accompanied her to the museum. Her humanitarian interest and concern endeared her to everyone who met her.

Next to visit us was the charming Queen Beatrix of the Netherlands, who arrived on 4 October, 1996. Dignitaries who accompanied her included Justice Minister Dullah

Noor with Queen Beatrice of the Netherlands at the District Six Museum on 4 October 1996

Omar. who was born in District Six. It was an opportunity for me to thank the Dutch government for their donation of R250 000 which was crucial to the establishment of the Museum.

In February 1997, King Carl Gustaf and Queen Silvia of Sweden honoured us with a visit. Sweden gave generous support to the liberation struggle in South Africa for many years, and has backed the District Six Museum since its establishment. We have "twinned" with the Malmo Museum in Sweden and are in constant contact with its staff.

Noor with King Gustav and Queen Sylvia of Sweden at the District Six Museum on 18 February 1997

A highlight, not only on the museum's calendar but also in my life occurred recently. Queen Sophia of Spain and her husband came to the museum with Graça Machel in February 1999. It was a wonderful event and both women were sympathetic and gracious. It was because of this that I had the temerity to ask Graça Machel to introduce me to our President, Mr Nelson Mandela, at a special reception which was being held at the Spanish Embassy that evening. The photograph opposite shows that the meeting took place. It was the culmination of my association with District Six.

Noor showing Queen Sophia of Spain and Graça Machel where he lived, during the visit of King Juan Carlos and Queen Sophia to the District Six Museum on 16 February 1999.

Noor with Nelson Mandela, Graça Machel and Queen Sophia of Spain, 16 February 1999

Acknowledgements

I would like to acknowledge my sincere gratitude to the Board of Trustees of the District Six Museum for publishing this book. Also to Cloete Breytenbach, Clarence Coulsen, George Hallett, Fakier Jessa, Johaar Mosaval, Salie Abed (Lobo) and Ridwaan Jattiem for kindly granting me permission to reproduce their photographs. And special thanks to Sandra Prosalendis, Linda Fortune, Colette Thorne, Patty Kolbe, Khalied Boltman, Haajirah Esau, Dammon Rice, Jos Thorne, Isgaak Ebrahim, Zerena Ebrahim and Mariam Ahmed for all their hard work in helping me.

This publication has been made possible by the generous donations to the District Six Museum of the Ford Foundation and Sida.